Cries of a Society

LaLa Speaks

LaVan Robinson

© Copyright October 2020 by Larry LaVan Richardson Jr. - All rights reserved.

> It is not legal to reproduce, duplicate, or transmit any part of this document in either electronic means or printed format. Recording of this publication is strictly prohibited.

ISBN: 9798559489476
Publisher: Independent Press

Editor: Lisa Tomey

Author Photo: Larry Richardson

Cover Photography: Tom Ritson on Unsplash

Internal Art: Unsplash as Credited

Author inquiries: Larry Richardson
writer7668@yahoo.com

U.S.A.

DEDICATION

First to God and all His glory as I publish this third book. To my family who are no longer of this earth, but in my heart. And to family in my life. To my son. For all who have believed in me. And for all who continue to pursue ways of peace.

Cries of a Society

CONTENTS

1 American Dream

3 Black is Beautiful

5 Book by the Cover

7 Brotherly Love

9 Bucket List

11 Cheers

12 Elation

13 Feast

15 Flowers

17 Focus

19 Grace

21 Hatred Flames

23 Illuminate

25 I'm Appalled

27 Lifeline

29 Magnificence

31 Melodies

33 Milk and Honey35 Miracle

37 Moment

39 Much More

41 Place

43 Playbook

45 Poetry

47 Praise

49 Preface

51 Raging Fires

53 Residuals

55 Script

57 Skin We're In

59 Storms

61 Swoon

63 The Agents of Chaos

65 Truth Will Set You Free

67 Twisted Tongue

69 Wasted Talent

71 Watch One Another's Backs

73 Worth

About the Author

Introduction

Step into the world of LaLa as he speaks of society from his poet mind's eye. Analytical, yet down to the basics of understanding the human condition in a society which is sometimes daunting. Yet, LaLa sees awareness as the path to understanding, leading to peaceful living. It is such hope that brings forth the consideration of change. That first step is within before it can ever be of the world. Let's read these words and inspire each of our own ways of thinking toward a common ground. LaLa puts down the hate as he picks up the pen

Photo by Takemaru Hirai on Unsplash

American Dream

Unfortunately, many lives are being lost to the pandemic daily. Politicians play out their agenda that turns out to be very, very costly. In the middle, the citizens are caught as no solutions to defeating this invisible adversary are visible or even sought. These are billionaires serving in public office and that's means for the working poor, putting nails in their coffin. For basic necessities people are vying and senselessly dying. Families are displaced and the children because of their very empty stomachs constantly crying. The same leaders in government are obligated and supposed to help relieve the unnecessary suffering and pain. They won't unless it's something for their cause to monetary gain. Therefore, many are left out in the pouring rain without hope to fend off the guilt and endless shame of not being able to for their family provide a safe and stable life or what it deems apart or a piece of the great American dream.

Photo by José on Unsplash

Black is Beautiful

In a world of uncertainty where lives of colored are placed in a deadly game of jeopardy. Being crucified because of the color of skin and despite the worldwide protests against this, it keeps happening over and over again. Leaders and people in power obsessed and pushing their agenda where it's all about obtaining more and more riches by the second, minutes and hour by hour. It's seems that no one seems to care about the carnage and pain the families have to forever carry and bear. Yes, it has to stop but I'm afraid it won't until the bomb they are preparing to on more innocent lives, they drop. Culminating in the fact that they know we're truly beautiful and since the beginning of time its full hatred on the culture of black.

Photo by Andrea Badino on Unsplash

Book by the Cover

Blessed with looks that are built to trance and even kill. Name in bold letters put in neon lights and featured on the A star list of bill. Appearing to be a rock of all ages that others can count and lean on. Wearing a paste on smile that's totally fake but troubling times have it overused, worn and from life's adversities with major turns. For them, the show must continue to go on. Despite even when the tragedies hit close to home. These brave souls give it their all even as they quietly inside filled with much pain and hurt suffer. Please don't judge these or anyone by the adage book by the cover

Photo by Humphrey Muleba on Unsplash

Brotherly Love

Oh, where I say where is amongst ourselves, brotherly love? Is it unattainable or is it just a concept we as a people always of it fall short of? In order for we as a nation to be from the grips of the past free. We must move on and fully embrace the spirit of love, peace, and unity. Maybe the psychological scars run deeper than expected and shouldn't under no circumstance be forgotten or neglected. We can't continue on it to dwell; we must learn from our mistakes or again face unforgettable actions that'll lead to the fiery depths of Hell. All it really takes is a warm, caring smile a handshake or even an unexpected hug to pass on to another brotherly love.

Cries of a Society

Photo by Mohamed Mohassi on Unsplash

Bucket List

The time has come where secrets will be no more. On this fact, the adversary will be acting and playing on its very core. The deadly game that they play will be on the center stage and in full display. Audiences around the world will be in total awe and captivated by the storyline that will outrightly sacrifice so many innocents' lives. Many will not be able to accept this new reality and their displeasure will cause them to take their fight and anger to the streets. Humanity will sink to a new low and by their actions. It'll reap what it sows. Blood in its streets will flow as retaliation for free expression spreads more rapidly and without boundaries grow. Is this the fate we will accept as answers to secrets no more will be hidden or kept? Brothers and sisters, we are so much better than this but scheming, chasing, and falling victim to follyness unfortunately is just another desirable pleasure that's written on humanity to do bucket list.

Photo by Matthew T Rader on Unsplash

Cheers

Every day I have to be mindful of the pitfalls that are willfully set in place to undermine my existence and take away the smile on my face, taking my soul to depths I otherwise dare not go. Daily struggling to break free from its vicious web of entanglement- knowing I'm not the first or last to face its fire and fury. Settling for the comfort of darkness and gloom anything to help quicken my internal place in misery and doom then suddenly the darkness subsides and starts to disappear, and the light of the sun ever so appears. A voice declares that the battle with this entity is fought and won so there's nothing to fear and from that moment my entrenched soul triumphantly stands tall praising God and Cheers.

Cries of a Society

Photo by Craig Whitehead on Unsplash

Elation

The boyz of privilege outright and boldly without conscious abusing their power. Totally aware that all that was sweet is soon bound to go bitter and sour knowing that their end time is near and as one last final stand, they're gonna manufacture what it seems like days and nights of unprecedented and perpetual fear. Fear not, for this too shall pass and when it's all said and done, love will be the only entity that will be triumphant and last. Standing tall in its principles and building a brand-new foundation where mankind praises God for the victory, singing and dancing lost in total elation.

Photo by Blogging Guide on Unsplash

Feast

Every day the one percent thru the politicians flex their muscles while their dirty and bloodstained dollars continue to fuel the devils hustle of the daily grind as the people are slowly slipping away and losing their integrity and minds. Unwilling victims of the power play that's slaying millions of innocents along the way. Getting high and drunk off the blood that they have spilled while celebrating the quota that they have met and continues to fill. This is the feast of the clever, conniving and lying beast while toasting that its way and lifestyle never cease.

Cries of a Society

Photo by Claudiu Morut on Unsplash

Flowers

Looking out from my window as the rain like a drum beats rapidly off my windowpane. I'm reminded that the blessings of the rain are the earth grounds are moistened and the seeds of love now properly nourished readily sprouts flowers and beauty along the worlds landscape solidifying its existence and destined place. Remember brothers and sisters, to bring out the beauty that's within you God has a detailed plan to brighten your horizon and will be there to see it manifested and properly through. Trust wholeheartedly in him and your flower too will add happiness and beauty to others as well as the earth when in full bloom.

Photo by Jilbert Ebrahimi on Unsplash

Focus

Twisted ideologies and bad decisions are a part of a society that among its citizens causing so much tension and great division. Hustling and grinding for a slice of prosperity where everyone is included in the pursuit of the American dream. The leaders make achieving this so dam hard by setting up obstacles both seen and unseen to make you purposely stumble and fall. When caught up in the act and lies, they just bold face deny, deny, and deny while in secrecy, busy tallying up the great dividends they get for each and every life. Off the backs of the embattled taxpayers and poor, they enjoy their lifestyles simple luxuries while the poor in their anguish gets to enjoy pain, strife, and misery. When it's in the leader's hands to share with the citizens the vast abundance of the resources with. They out of rebuttal claim to not or want anything to do with it. Leaving many desperate, distraught, and utterly hopeless. Wondering for them and their families where their next meal will come from or where they'll lay their heads under the sun being that this is their only and main focus.

Photo by Tony Eight Media on Unsplash

Grace

In his image we were divinely created. The greatest of all his masterpieces that God himself was pleased and elated. Putting mankind high upon the creator's pedestal. Providing him with all the essential and necessary tools to accomplish and persevere through this journey called life. Equipped with boundless potential and free will to know the difference between wrong and right. Somewhere along the way, mankind fell off course and track. Relying upon himself, refusing God whom he boldly on turned his back. God is love and love forgives, and it is only by the blessing of his mercy and grace that despite all this, mankind is still able to exist and live.

Cries of a Society

Photo by Cullan Smith on Unsplash

Hatred Flames

Citizens are struggling every day to survive and to this basic fact, leaders are completely blind. They're taking their anger to the streets and lashing out against all and who they come upon and meet. Wanting so badly for their voices to be heard and needing a helping hand. Times are tough because there is no love for themselves and their fellow man. There is so much division among us and it's a real shame. We all need to take a long deep look inside ourselves and be accountable and take some of the blame. The more things change the more they continue to stay the same. We as one humanity must put aside the nonsense and come together before it's too late and this world of ours burn into oblivion from the flames of hate.

Photo by Anne Nygård on Unsplash

Illuminate

In a word that's filled with so much darkness, misery, pain, and despair. Each and everyone here have been given a unique and special gift within to unconditionally share. To bring validity to the existence of the soul's true purpose and being. To the fullest able to pursue life's wonders and mysteries. Praising God from where all true strength lies and resonates. Being able to just with a warm smile and caring touch. Elevating one another so they too can illuminate.

Photo by Clay Banks on Unsplash

I'm Appalled

The boyz are bigots in disguise and their involvement in nefarious groups, they do participate with such honor and pride. Their motto is to shoot first and ask questions last just like they used to do to our ancestors in the not so distant past. This is the new operating procedure that's law. It's all for one and one for all as many innocent lives because of this action every day to it simply fall. Executing brothers and sisters boldly like animals to slaughter backed by a system who relishes in its delights watching citizens' falter. I am appalled by such actions that they show they hate us with so much passion. Why is this so? Please somebody let me know what is their daily goal?!!!! No don't tell me this we all can see, and I'm appalled as their mission is to annihilate people that look like both you and me.

Photo by Nicholas Barbaros on Unsplash

Lifeline

I was drowning in the massive sea of hopelessness and despair. I was yelling and crying out for help, but it seemed like no one could hear me and or even cared. Many passed by but wouldn't help and I questioned, doubted and in my pity starting to lose my very essence of self. Wow, many thought I was a goner because by their definition, I was a miserable loner. Misery was my-I admit- constant bedfellow following me fronting everywhere I go. It felt like a weight I just couldn't get off my thin and fragile shoulders. More and more daily it became me against what I was wanting and terribly yearning for, yes, love and I grew colder and colder. So, I decided to jump into the sea motionless not even struggling to the bottom just quickly sinking. Realizing what I had done, thoughts of surviving ran all throughout my mind. Just then you suddenly appeared with love, smiling, armed with warm hugs, blankets and to my prayers, providing a much wanted, needed, and appreciated lifeline.

Photo by Simon Berger on Unsplash

Magnificence

Love is an entity that can entrance many types of emotions that runneth within us like a stream into the vast ocean.

It can adapt to any situation we may face. Healing powers so extraordinary that pain and misery of them both won't even be a trace.

We are the beauty of its end results brought into validation so its essence can be seen and felt.

So be willing and able to heed and humble yourself to its wonderful call from the Heavenly Father above who loves us so very, very much to unconditionally share his grace and magnificence amongst us all.

Photo by Anne Nygård on Unsplash

Melodies

In the darkest moments, the brightest light shines. Bringing clarity and insightfulness to the spiritual conscious and mind. Strength abounding from the creative within giving validity of the essential elements that allow freedom to take form and begin the naturalization of life to harmonize the binding of the heart, mind, and soul. Revealing musical melodies and lyrics yearning to be discovered and told.

Photo by Charl Folscher on Unsplash

Milk and Honey

In this land of milk and honey. There's nothing more important to the corrupt leaders except for finding elaborate schemes to keep raking in their pockets the taxpayers hard earned money. The benefits of public service are that once in office, the enticement and seduction of the outright maniacal manipulation of resources evidently to them is totally worth it. Sacrificing their all to enjoy to the fullest and reap the benefits just before from their self-greed and willful pride, they like dominoes one after one tragically and politically fall. Of course, meanwhile in the interim, innocent souls are destroyed as they set up dummy corporations to funnel the money to posing as legitimate businesses but in reality, they're just decoys. For so long, this, and more has been happening. So please brothers and sisters, take heed to this long-standing practice because the effects on us all is just so dam heartfelt and saddening. This is not at least or anyway funny while living, struggling, and dying in this land of milk and honey.

Cries of a Society

Photo by Dewang Gupta on Unsplash

Miracle

You're the one Lord that has made me who I am today and in all I say and do. I will give you the praise. All will see by my works of faith that in you, I dwell and that your love, mercy, and grace has saved my soul from the depths of Hell. I will draw men unto you so from God himself, they can experience the miracle too.

Photo by Jeremy Bishop on Unsplash

Moment

We all will have a moment where we must either decide to embrace it or not take it. This is our time to shine illuminating that which is in you to validation each and every time. Your inner drive to be and do the very best will be put to criticism and life's ongoing and never-ending tests. Remember you are a part of something that is great and don't let your own understanding and council decide your fate. Rely on God and life's storms at that defining moment, he'll see you safely through standing always proudly with and beside you.

Cries of a Society

Photo by Louis Smit on Unsplash

Much More

It's a two-party system with the illusion of choice. The sum of both evils where you still have no voice. You vote them in power as they behind closed doors plot to take away your freedoms hour by the hour. They want it all for themselves and they really couldn't give a damn about you or anyone else. Money is their God and illegally gained or gotten as they continue boldly their agenda on innocent souls to masterfully manipulate spiritually, mentally, and physically the downtrodden. So, brothers and sisters if you're not at all happy with what's in our world is going on. There's so much you can definitely do. Stand up for what's yours because you deserve so much more though and through.

Photo by Ross Findon on Unsplash

Place

To be judged and hated for who I am and being treated less than a man and human. Living in a country that wholeheartedly and out rightly despises my ancestors and future generations of people that look like me. Rewarding my frustrations and fight for equality for which I am peacefully standing up for my civil rights and acceptance with violence and hellish brutality. Laws and institutions enacted to separate and willfully divide and to exterminate purposely whole races of innocent souls and lives. I've come to the conclusion that of the benefits of this great country they have used by any means necessary, the act and power of exclusion. America, I do humbly plea, what truly is it that you want from me? I forgave you and have turned constantly the other cheek and time and time again, without conscious, you have continuously downtrodden, oppressed and offended me. I don't know how much more of this I can possibly take so I ask once again America what would you do if it was reversed and you were in my place?

Cries of a Society

Photo by Jon Tyson on Unsplash

Playbook

In this elaborate game of give and take. It's war between the entities as humanity lifestyles and lives are at stake. All we have accomplish will not matter as the foundations of society and its ideologies like dust in the wind starting to falter and are widely scattered. There are rules that must be abided but in war, there's no fair play and which side to fight for, many are confused and divided. Waking up to another day where their everyday visions and dreams are by selfishness and greed by the politicians and rich game plan are so very devastated by leaving them horrifically shook from the devious play calling by the adversary and their evil playbook.

Cries of a Society

Photo by Trust "Tru" Katsande on Unsplash

Poetry

When all else fails, Poetry speaks, providing a path to self-awareness which gives strength to the weak. Poetry gives manifestation to mankind's deepest desires and wisdom to quench his souls burning fires. Providing a clear and precise path to spiritual insight completing the binding and taking mankind to unprecedented heights.

Photo by Shane Rounce on Unsplash

Praise

Every morning I wake up grateful that another day has arrived and despite the darkness over the horizon that looms, the sun continues to brightly shine. My lungs being filled with God given breath and he is there to comfort me and wipe away from my eyes and face, the many tears I have wept. The chance to one again get down on my knees giving him praise for all the wonderful ways he continues to show that he loves me. Giving me strength and hope to continue when I feel that I just can't anymore and enduring evilness against me that have formed. Shielding me from the hurt and pain associated with life's tragedies and turbulent storms. Yes, to you Heavenly Father, I life my voice and arms in praise grateful for the chance to see and do this another glorious day.

Cries of a Society

Photo by Sunyu on Unsplash

Preface

Looking out upon the massive sea of different buy similar faces and realizing that mankind is represented by all its many, many races. Wanting basically the same thing. The pursuit of love, peace, and happiness and the joys that having such so, so brings. We are all here and made for a specific purpose and to find it though, you must look deep inside the mere surface. Pray, trust God, and keep the faith. When you find you gift, share and better the world allowing your identity to take preface.

Photo by Adam Wilson on Unsplash

Raging Fires

Situations dictate how most people think or act. Right now, the events that are happening in the world around us got people in the mode of attack. Leaders can't or refuse to help because they're a big part of the problem as many are just trying to stay afloat and not hit rock bottom. Everywhere they seemed lost and confused, not having any direction or even know what to do. Grasping for air as these events and the recoil from such of, they just can't no more bear. Giving up hope and turning against their own. Perpetrating actions that by normal standards can't be from their state of mind, condoned. Falling victim to their own selfish understanding and desires just constantly adding more daily fuel to the already inferno raging fires.

Cries of a Society

Photo by Sharon McCutcheon on Unsplash

Residuals

To love is the greatest gift one can to another freely give. For it is meant to add substance and meaning to the way we all live. It is not to be contained. Adding value to what here on earth, we spiritually, mentally, and physically gain. Providing strength and hope when all seem lost. Compromising and even willing to sacrifice to uplift one's soul at any cost. Overall making one a much better individual immediately and long after while basking in loves undying and intangible residuals.

Cries of a Society

Photo by Priscilla Du Preez on Unsplash

Script

The soul of America is at stake as the corrupt government is and has for so long been on the take. Selling souls like that of market and pushing strong their agenda and zeroing in on the projected target. Destroying households and neighborhoods with malice and devious intent overwhelmingly while on unnecessary frivolous items, taxpayer's money is foolishly spent. Greed is the blueprint that the foundation is built on while terror is unleashed and practiced in many forms. Their future in evil hands shaped like putty and clay and with new leadership sticking to the negotiated preordained script, nothing will drastically change. It'll get worse before it gets better, this we all can see but we all have the power to make this world of ours a home that promotes love, peace and for all humanity unity.

Photo by Annie Spratt on Unsplash

Skin We're In

This generation is ruthless and full of hatred and bigotry. They are determined to destroy themselves and all of humanity. Falling into the set traps because of refusal to gain knowledge of self they so lack. Believing that tooting a gun makes them a big person. Fitting the stereotypical role perfectly without even rehearsing. The leaders and law makers like this system the way it is set up. Brothers and sisters killing one another, for them it's never enough. They claim it's not their problem so they're not in a hurry to find or offer solutions to solve them. So please brothers and sisters, this we have the power to end by spreading goodwill amongst ourselves and appreciate and love the skin we're in.

Cries of a Society

Photo by J W on Unsplash

Storms

After going through the storm, I realized life as I knew it had drastically changed. All of my materialistic possessions were either gone, destroyed, or totally rearranged. I got on my knees grateful to God that I had survived and given another chance to take inventory of my life. Now the little things I've learned to appreciate like spreading love and goodwill among men because time is precious and for no one will wait. So, make good use of all you possess and have. Spreading joy and happiness to days that are sad. Be grateful. Praise God and even though storms may come causing temporary confusion. You have the power to re-write a much better and brighter conclusion.

Cries of a Society

Photo by Brett Jordan on Unsplash

The Agents of Chaos

Everyone who comes into your life isn't there to bring you joy. They parade around promoting peace when that's just a decoy for the mission at hand and that's to destroy the essence of man. They're able to assume many faces as they infiltrate the races. Their agenda is plain and clear which is to cause mass hysteria and instill fear. Playing their role for all that it's worth, slowly but surely manifesting their playground, Hell on Earth. Just look around and you can't help but to see all the fuss being caused by the agents of chaos.

Photo by Markus Winkler on Unsplash

Truth Will Set You Free

The inhabitants of the slippery tongue boldly lie to your faces as they go all out to cause tensions among the races. For their purpose, twisting the facts because this is for them a serious knack. Hoping that the citizens remain clueless and blind as they tighten their grips on the feeble minds. Claiming that you have a choice to make it once again better. It won't until we as humanity take a stand against negativity together. See through beyond the countless lies because the truth will set you free and will never die.

Cries of a Society

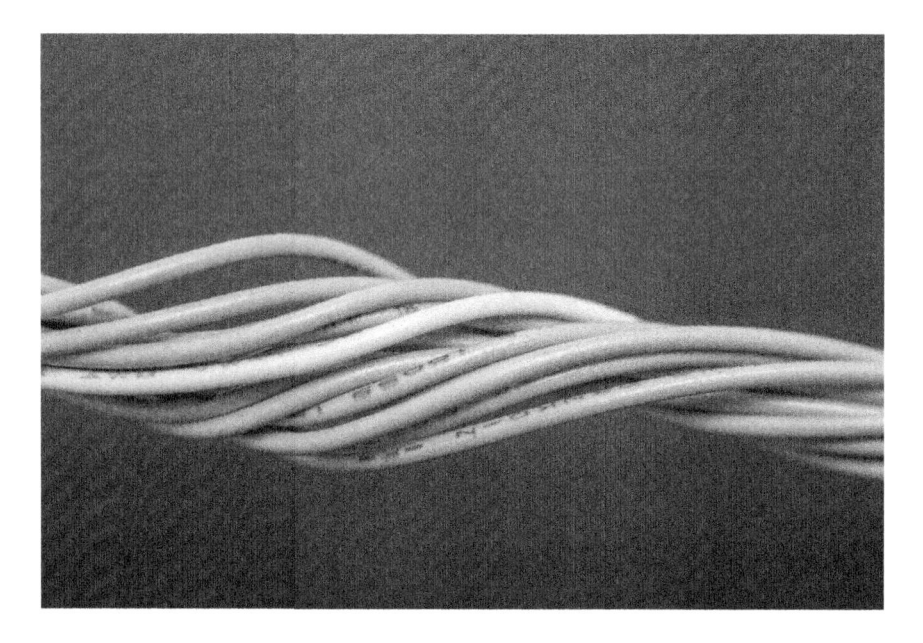

Photo by Steve Johnson on Unsplash

Twisted Tongue

Watch what the leaders do not what they equivalently say because their stories and lies change, but actions remain the same. Only caring for the survival of themselves and having no sympathy or empathy for you or anyone else. Getting lost and full off their selfishness while souls are lost and written off as a business expense. Smiling in your face as they position the dagger in your back to lodge deep in place. Brothers and sisters be careful of their twisted tongue. Making promises on top of promises that's not kept under the rays of the sun. Keeping you confused is what they behind closed doors pray that they continue to do. Setting you up in this game called life not to win but to lose, lose, and lose.

Photo by Etienne Girardet on Unsplash

Wasted Talent

We all have gifts that are meant for the spirit to uplift. The world would be a much better place if we didn't let our desires and wants take control and get in our way. Causing the average person to lose his/her integrity, become materialistic and egotistical filled with selfish pride. Always in clashes with what the Father in heaven truly has ordained to make our purpose here on earth valid. Take time to find who you really are and don't end up becoming wasted talent.

Cries of a Society

Photo by Nicolas Picard on Unsplash

Watch One Another's Backs

The onslaught attack on all of humanity has been greatly intensified and it includes all lives. No one is safe from this madness as it stretches its agenda across the globe bringing pain, misery, and unprecedented sadness. While people's attentions are carefully, methodically, and well-coordinated elsewhere. The cohorts of destruction continue to perpetrate and systemically manufacture terror and fear here. Boldly, knowing that their time to wreak havoc on earth is short and coming to an end. There is nothing as you can hopefully see that they wouldn't do to capture the souls of men. Beware of the traps and definitely watch one another backs.

Photo by Alfred Aloushy on Unsplash

Worth

The power that you inside possess has already endured life and times test. You are the manifestation of what can be achieved when you properly channel it for good and by faith truly believe. Your potential is of great heights guided by tone and wisdom and its valuable and intangible insights. So, let not anything here on this earth dictate what you really are worth.

Cries of a Society

ABOUT THE AUTHOR

LaVan Robinson, born as Larry LaVan Richardson, Jr, took his pen name from his middle name and his mother Mary's maiden name. He writes in her honor. As well, he has a beloved son, Audy. A 13 year veteran, he has written poetry since high school. In January he published his first poetry book, Songs of LaLA, followed by his second book Love's Rhapsody. "LaLa" is Robinson's poet name. He states that he loves poetry and will use it to inspire people and bring them closer to God. You can find LaLa performing at open mic's and on podcasts.

Cries of a Society

Other Books by LaVan Robinson

Songs of LaLa: The Poet which was released as a second edition in 2020 and Love's Rhapsody, published in 2020 both available on Amazon.

Cries of a Society

Cries of a Society

Printed in Great Britain
by Amazon